—Weird and Wacky Science—

# BIZARRE INSECTS

Margaret J. Anderson

ENSLOW PUBLISHERS, INC.

44 Fadem Road
Box 699
Springfield, N.J. 07081
U.S.A.

P.O. Box 38
Aldershot
Hants GU12 6BP
U.K.

*To the bug hunters:*
*Alex, Casey, Cam, Chris, Connor, and Jena Rose*

**Library of Congress Cataloging-in-Publication Data**

Anderson, Margaret Jean, 1931–
 Bizarre Insects / by Margaret J. Anderson.
  p. cm. — (Weird and wacky science)
 Includes bibliographical references and index.
 ISBN 0-89490-613-5
 1. Insects—Miscellanea—Juvenile literature. [1. Insects.]
 I. Title. II. Series.
 QL467.2.A514 1996
 595.7—dc20                                    94-23725
                                                    CIP
                                                    AC

Printed in the United States of America

10 9 8 7 6 5 4 3 2 1

**Illustration Credits**: Margaret J. Anderson, pp. 8, 15, 28, 42; Enslow Publishers, Inc., pp. 12, 20, 31; Jeffrey G. Miller, 11, 18, 36; Montana State University Archives, p. 34; Sallie Bowman, p. 25, Thomas Eisner, 32; Visuals Unlimited: © Walt Anderson, p. 39; © C.P. Hickman, p. 22; © Kjell B. Sandved, p. 17; © W.J. Weber, p. 4.

**Cover Illustration**: Lantern bug (Sabeh, Malaysia), ©Michael Fogden/Animals, Animals.

# Contents

This successful insect has been around since before the days of the dinosaurs.

# ☀ 1 ☀

# WEIRD INSECTS

The weird creature moved easily in the darkness. It returned to the place where it had found the body yesterday and began to eat. Its heavy jaws moved sideways. Its flat body was completely encased in armor. The warm damp basement was filled with its musty smell.

A sudden bright light startled the creature. It raised its smooth face. The light dazzled its hundred eyes, but it had nothing to fear. It was a survivor. Its kind had been around for millions of years. Then a huge hand reached down and snatched its meal away by the tail. With a whir of noise, the creature spread its wings and flew back into the darkness. It clung to the wall where it had landed. The beam of light found it again, and it scuttled away. Turning sideways, it slipped into an impossibly narrow crack in the wall.

What do you think the creature was?

Something in a horror movie.

An alien from outer space.

An animal left over from dinosaur times.

A cockroach.

All of the above.

If you picked all of the above, you are right!

Insects often give scriptwriters ideas for horror movies. They give science-fiction writers ideas for invading aliens. Insects are really weird creatures. It's lucky for us that they are all quite small, or they would have taken over the earth long ago. They already outweigh humans by three hundred to one.[1] For every pound of human flesh in the world, there are three hundred pounds of insects.

Insects have been around for a long time. Take the cockroach, for example. Cockroaches have hardly changed in the last 200 million years. Even before the age of dinosaurs, they crawled through the warm, damp, prehistoric forests. Now they roam around warm, damp basements. They weren't choosy about what they ate back then; and they aren't choosy about what they eat today.

## Strength and Protection

For its size, an insect is incredibly strong. The tough outer skin is called an exoskeleton, which means "skeleton on the outside." An insect's strength comes from having its muscles joined to large areas of the exoskeleton. If you could jump like a grasshopper, you would be able to clear a football field in one leap. An ant can carry a load four times its own weight in its jaws. That's like you picking up a three- or four-hundred-pound weight with your teeth.

An insect's exoskeleton is a bit like the armor worn by knights back in the fifteenth century. Of course a knight's muscles were not attached to his armor, so he had trouble getting around, and even had to be lifted onto his horse. Armor was very hot and uncomfortable to wear. Even on a cold day, the knight was soaked in sweat. He also had a hard time breathing when his visor was down.

An insect doesn't have a perspiration problem. It is cold blooded. Its body temperature goes up and down with the temperature of its surroundings. It doesn't have a breathing problem, although it has neither a nose nor lungs. Instead it has spiracles, or air holes, along the sides of its body that lead to breathing tubes.

## Molting

An exoskeleton has a lot of advantages when it comes to strength and safety. However, it has one big disadvantage. It cannot grow. Our inside skeletons add more bone and grow along with us. That doesn't work if your skeleton is on the outside.

So how does an insect get bigger? It has to molt or shed its hard skeleton. It molts anywhere from three to twenty times, depending on the kind of insect. Underneath the old skin is a new, soft skin that lets the insect's body expand. The new exoskeleton slowly hardens. This is a high-risk time for the insect. While the exoskeleton is still soft, the insect cannot fly or run away from its enemies.

Until the new skin is hard, it cannot support much weight.

This limits the size to which an insect can grow. The movies have it all wrong when they show flies or spiders the size of cats or dogs. There's no way a fly could grow to be that big; it would burst during molting.

The exoskeleton completely covers the insect. It covers its antennae, or feelers, and lines its breathing tubes. The exoskeleton even covers its eyes.

Insects see a different world than we do. That's not just because they are small; it's because of their strange eyes. Because each eye has hundreds of lenses, insects don't see details. However, their

Insects have to shed their hard exoskeletons as they grow. This hissing cockroach will soon be as dark as its old skin.

eyes are great for detecting movement. That's why it's so hard to swat a fly.

## Big Changes

Sometimes big changes happen between one molt and the next. A butterfly, for example, starts out as an egg. Then it becomes a caterpillar; then a chrysalis; and finally an adult butterfly. This way of growing is called metamorphosis, which means "change of shape." Some insects, such as grasshoppers, go through incomplete metamorphosis. Young grasshoppers look like their parents, but they are smaller and don't have wings.

## Strange Ways

Insects often behave in weird ways. Female praying mantises have been known to eat their mates. A hungry mother insect sometimes gobbles up her own children. This is usually a case of mistaken identity, however. Those hundred eyes are not good for recognizing faces, and there's an added problem when the kids don't look like their parents.

Some insects go to a lot of trouble to make life easy for the next generation. One kind of small wasp makes sure her little grubs don't go hungry by laying her eggs inside fat caterpillars. When the wasp eggs hatch, the grubs are surrounded by their favorite food—caterpillar guts! A grub is careful not to be too greedy. It likes its food fresh, so it doesn't kill off its host right away. It just nibbles the caterpillar's insides, while the caterpillar is nibbling leaves. The caterpillar spins a cocoon, but what finally comes out is not a colorful butterfly. By this time the caterpillar has been devoured, and a small wasp emerges.

## Good and Bad Insects

It takes a lot of food to satisfy the billions and billions of insects that share our world. When an insect lives on our food, we call it a "bad" insect. We don't like finding a grub in an ear of corn. We call an insect that destroys the grub that eats our food a "good" insect. Insect parasites, like the wasp that grows up inside a caterpillar, are good. (A parasite is an animal that gets food and a place to live inside another animal.) Insect predators, or meat eaters, are also good when their prey is pest insects. Insect parasites and predators are on our side in the struggle to keep ahead of the plant eaters. Insects that pollinate flowers are also good insects. Without them we would not have most kinds of fruits and vegetables.

The insects that end up being eaten are an important link in the food chain. They provide a valuable source of protein for many species of birds, mammals, and fish. In some places, insects are included in the human diet. In Africa, several kinds of insects and grubs are considered good eating. In Nepal, bakuti, a paste made from mashed bee pupae, is a big favorite. Bakuti looks rather like scrambled eggs and has a nutty taste. In the Western world, we don't like the thought of eating bugs, but to make better use of the world's resources, it might be a good idea to find ways to make insects appetizing.[2] Anyone for a bee burger and French flies?

The eyes of a robber fly are good for detecting movement. Each eye has hundreds of lenses.

Lantern flies are bugs with weird heads. In spite of their name, they do not light up.

# ✴2✴

# THE UGLY INSECT CONTEST

If you were judging an Ugly Insect Contest, you would be likely to give extra points for size. As far as insects go, big is ugly. Ugly is also scary. When an insect is big, you can't help noticing all six of its legs. You can't help noticing its spines, bristles, antennae, flapping wings, and bug eyes.

Midges and crane flies look a lot like each other. Both are ugly insects, but midges are so small you can hardly see them. They wouldn't get many points in the Ugly Insect Contest. Crane flies, on the other hand, are big. You can't miss their long dangling legs. Crane flies flop about as if they don't know where they are going. Even though they're harmless, you wouldn't want one to fly into your face. Adult crane flies look better to us than their children. A young crane fly is a large gray blob of a grub. It has no legs, and it has so little shape that it's hard to tell its head from its tail end. It hides in the mud in the bottom of a pond or stream.

## Walkingsticks

The Australian walkingstick is another big, ugly insect. It does its best not to be noticed. Like many insects, it is camouflaged so that it blends into its surroundings. That's not easy when you are almost six inches long and have a large, plump, spiny body. When a walkingstick is scared, it sways gently, trying to look like a dry leaf shaking in the wind. It often curves up its tail end. If its enemies don't think it's a leaf, maybe they'll think that it stings like a scorpion. The fierce look is all bluff, though. Walkingsticks don't sting or bite. All they've got going for them is ugliness. The little ones don't even have that protection. When walkingsticks are small, they are actually rather cute.

The female walkingstick is too fat to fly; her wings are small flaps. The male is much skinnier than the female, and he does have wings. He uses them to cruise around in search of a mate. To him, females are neither fat nor ugly.

## Ugly Beetles

The goliath beetle, as you might guess from its name, is another insect giant—an ugly giant with a long snout. It is around ten inches long and acts more like a bird than like an insect. It lives in Africa, so you're not likely to have one zoom in and land on you. If one does, stay calm; goliath beetles only eat fruit.

The rhinoceros beetle has a big snout. The female burrows into wood. She gives off a scent that attracts male beetles. If two males show up at the same time, they wrestle with their strong mouthparts, and they fight to the death. In Thailand, beetle

In Thailand, people place bets on the outcome of fights between male rhinoceros beetles.

fighting is a national sport. People stage fights and bet on which beetle will be the winner.

Compared with its giant cousins, the bombardier beetle is quite small, but it does have a weird and ugly way of protecting itself. It uses chemical warfare. When a bombardier beetle senses danger, it lowers its tail end between its legs and shoots out a cloud

**15**

of poison gas, which can kill other insects. The gas can also burn skin and leaves a brown stain. If you're close enough, you can hear a little pop. It sounds like a living cannon. Most bombardiers get off no more than four or five shots before recharging, but Thomas Eisner at Cornell University once met up with a twenty-nine-shooter.[1]

## The Ugly Queen

Another ugly thing about insects is the way they move. They scuttle . . . or dart . . . or flutter. However, the insect that wins the most points in the Ugly Insect Contest, the termite queen, doesn't move at all. Termites are social insects; several kinds live together in a nest—soldiers, workers, kings, and queens. The queen is really just an egg-laying machine, laying as many as eight thousand eggs in a single day. In Africa, one kind of termite queen has a huge pale body the size of a potato. You can tell she's an insect by the tiny head and six legs sticking out of one end. She never goes anywhere; her legs are far too small to support the weight of her big potato body. Plus, the tunnels in the nest are too narrow for her to squeeze through. The queen is a life prisoner in her royal home, and she serves a long sentence. Some termite queens live for fifty years.

## Losers in the Ugly Contest

One insect that wouldn't get many points in the Ugly Insect Contest is the butterfly. The butterfly's beauty is a kind of protection. Birds are warned off by its bright colors. To a bird, the eyespots on the wings of a peacock butterfly look like owl eyes. The orange and black of the monarch butterfly's wings are warning colors. Birds have found out that monarchs taste awful. Viceroy butterflies look like

The termite queen never moves. The termite workers and soldiers do all the work of burrowing the tunnels of the nest.

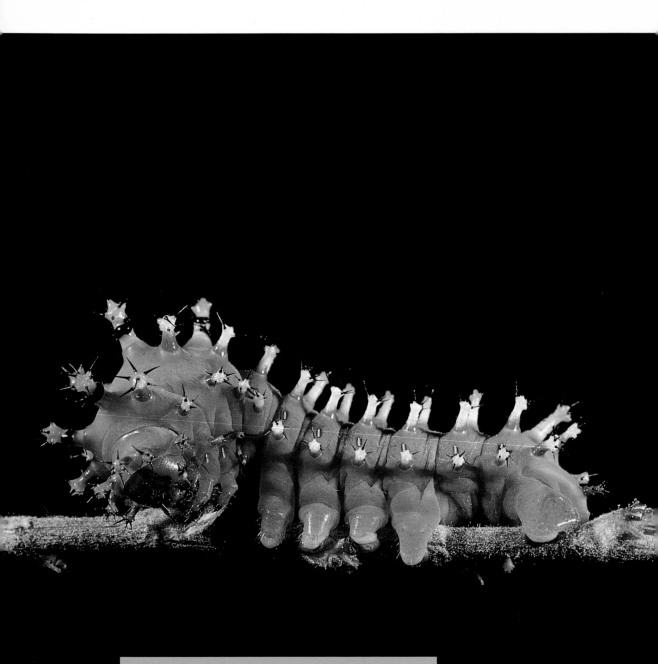

This caterpillar might not win the Ugly Insect Contest, but it is ugly enough to scare off birds.

monarchs, but they don't taste bad. Birds don't eat viceroy butterflies, either.

Some caterpillars use bright colors as a protection. When the pussmoth caterpillar is scared, it rears up its head end to show a vivid red patch and false eyes. It has a whiplike tail, and looks more like a monster than like a tasty caterpillar. A bird that meets a pussmoth backs off and looks elsewhere for its next meal.

In the insect world, it's better to be ugly than beautiful. Other animals mostly leave ugly insects alone, and that's what ugly insects want. They want to be left alone so that they can produce more insects that are just as ugly as they are.

A shield bug nymph. Bugs are a special kind of insect that belong to the order Hemiptera.

# 3

# DIRTY AND DEADLY

Entomologists are scientists who study insects. Only a few chase butterflies with nets, and only a few study bugs. Even though we often call insects "bugs," all insects are not bugs—but all the bugs that entomologists study are insects.

Entomologists divide insects into big groups called orders to help keep track of the millions of different kinds. All the members of an order have something in common that separates them from insects in other orders. Bugs, for example, belong to the order Hemiptera. In all bugs, the front half of the upper pair of wings is tough and leathery. Hemiptera comes from the Greek words *hemi* (half) and *ptera* (wing).

Bugs have sucking mouthparts. Some, like the bed bug, suck blood. Others, like the stink bug, live on plant juices. If you ever have the misfortune to bite into a raspberry with a stink bug

A blowfly feeds on meat. These nasty insects lay their eggs in open wounds.

hiding in it, you'll know how it got its name! Birds leave stink bugs alone.

**Flies**

When entomologists talk about flies, they are talking about insects that belong to another order, Diptera. True flies have only two wings—a single pair. The name Diptera comes from the Greek words for "two" and "wing." (Except for those insects that don't have any wings, all others have four wings.)

Flies have a weird habit of laying their eggs in places where no self-respecting creature would want its kids to grow up: manure piles; dead meat; living meat. It's disgusting when the living meat is a cow or a horse. It's even worse when the living meat is a person!

The horse botfly spends its young stages inside—you guessed it—a horse. The female lays her eggs among the hairs on a horse's front legs. The eggs stay there for weeks, or even months, until the horse licks itself. The moment it does, the eggs hatch. The tiny maggots quickly burrow into the tongue, living inside it for a month. Then they pop out and are swallowed. They spend the next nine months in the horse's gut.

The human botfly doesn't get on people the same way, because people don't lick themselves clean. The female hangs around a marsh and lays her eggs on a mosquito. When the mosquito lands on a person, the warmth of the body is a signal for the botfly eggs to hatch. The little creatures burrow into the skin, or they may take the easy way in through the mosquito bite.

About fifty years ago, a scientist named Lawrence Dunn learned about the history of the botfly the hard way.[1] He reared botflies from eggs—two in his left arm, two in his right arm, and two in his right leg. The place where the maggot went in itched and became very red and swollen. Dunn took careful notes. Pretty soon he had boils full of blood and pus on his arms and leg. After forty-six days, full-grown maggots began to pop out. They measured an inch long and a third of an inch around. Dunn then wrote a scientific paper about his discovery.

Another nasty insect is the blowfly, which lays its eggs in open wounds. The maggots live on pus. Even though having the blowfly maggots in a wound sounds disgusting, they actually help it to heal more quickly. During World War I, blowfly maggots were used to clean soldiers' wounds. Great numbers were reared for this purpose. Luckily for us, scientists discovered that the wounds heal faster because the maggots produce a chemical called allantoin. So we can now skip the maggots and just use allantoin to speed up healing.

## The House Fly

Botflies and blowflies cause a lot of problems, but there is another kind of fly that is much more dangerous. It's an insect that everyone knows, but few of us fear. It doesn't bite or sting. This insect, which belongs right up there on the Most Wanted Insect list (or *Least* Wanted), is none other than the common house fly. House flies have very dirty habits. They can carry millions of bacteria, spreading terrible diseases, such as cholera, typhoid, leprosy, and polio.

House flies are middle-sized flies. Tiny fruit flies and huge buzzing bluebottles also show up in houses. Fruit flies, house flies, and bluebottles are all different kinds of adult flies. Small flies do not grow into big flies. Like other insects, flies go through metamorphosis, meaning "change of form." There are four forms, or stages, in all: egg, maggot, pupa, and adult.

The female house fly lays her eggs in a pile of manure, which is warm and rich in nutrients. That makes it a good place to grow up in (if you are a fly). The eggs hatch into little white maggots. The maggots, surrounded by warm, rich food, grow quickly. In a week, they are eight hundred times heavier than when they hatched. (If humans grew this fast, a week-old baby would weigh

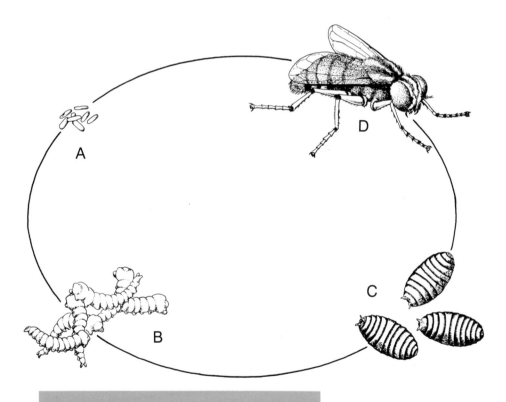

A
B
C
D

The four stages in the life cycle of a house fly: egg, maggot, pupa, adult.

three tons!) The maggot turns into a pupa, its resting stage. In about a week, it becomes an adult house fly.

An adult house fly can live for as long as two months. That's quite a long time for an insect. Mayflies, for example, live for only a few hours as adults. In the house fly's lifetime, it samples a lot of different kinds of food. House flies don't have biting mouthparts. That's where the trouble starts. Because they cannot chew, everything they eat must be liquid. When a fly lands on your peanut butter sandwich, the first thing it does is spit on it. Fly spit is so strong that it turns solids to liquids, so the fly can then drink some sandwich. A little spit is usually left behind. The spit contains some of the fly's last meal, which could have been a dead rat or dog droppings. Flies are not picky eaters, maybe because they grew up in a manure pile. They'll eat anything from a cow pie to apple pie.

A fly's long life gives it lots of time to lay eggs. If all the eggs from one pair of flies hatched into maggots, and all the maggots lived to have offspring, within a summer the original pair of flies would have about half a million grandchildren.[2] Luckily for us, most eggs and maggots don't make it. They get eaten, or they are killed off by bad weather or fly diseases.

Henry Ford was not a doctor, but he did a lot to improve our nation's health. Ford made the first mass-produced cars. Can you figure out how this could make us healthier?

Flies are the clue. Before there were cars, people got around on horseback. More horses meant more manure. More manure meant more flies. Flies caused outbreaks of disease. Cars cause air pollution and accidents (or their drivers do), but they don't spread cholera or typhoid.

## Mosquitoes and Malaria

Malaria is another disease that was a big killer until people knew how it was spread. Long ago, it was called swamp fever, because people thought the disease came from damp places. They were right, but it wasn't the damp that made people sick. It was the bite of another member of the order of Diptera—the mosquito.

Like house flies, mosquitoes live long enough to lay several batches of eggs. Before a female lays a batch of eggs, she needs a meal of blood, which she gets by tapping into someone's vein. If she bites a person who is sick with malaria, she sucks in malaria parasites along with the blood. She passes these parasites to the next person she bites. Only the female mosquito is dangerous; the male doesn't need a blood meal.

Malaria parasites spend part of their life cycle in human blood.[3] They spend the rest of their life cycle in a mosquito. It's weird that even though we are millions of times bigger and tougher than a mosquito, we are the ones who get sick. Mosquitoes carry the parasite, but they don't get malaria.

Honey bees do not sting while they are swarming. You wouldn't want to try this with killer bees!

# ✳ 4 ✳

# GANG WARFARE

**M**ost insects only take care of themselves, but there are some, called social insects, that depend on one another. They live in a group home. They cannot survive away from the group for long. Ants and honey bees are good examples. Killer bees are also social insects, even though, from our point of view, their behavior is antisocial.

Killer bees get a lot of bad press. Even their name sounds deadly. One killer bee is nothing to worry about. Its sting is no worse than the sting of a honey bee. A few thousand stings are a different matter, and that's where the problem lies. Killer bees attack in gangs.

Killer bees look a lot like normal honey bees. Even an entomologist has a hard time telling a dead killer bee from a dead honey bee. Killer bees tend to be a little smaller, and they also have slightly shorter tongues. Because bees from the same nest or hive vary in size, you need to measure the bodies and tongues of a lot of bees to be sure you've got killer bees.

With live bees, however, it is a different story. You can tell them apart by the way they act. "Busy as a bee" takes on a whole new meaning when it refers to killer bees. Killer bees are workaholics. They get up early and go to bed late. Sometimes they even work by moonlight. Killer-bee queens lay more eggs and lay them faster than honey-bee queens do. Killer bees defend their territory more fiercely. That's how they got the name "killer." Killer bees gang up on anything that disturbs their nest. They don't care if its people, pets, or wild animals.

Entomologists call killer bees African or Africanized bees.[1] Forty years ago, a scientist brought some African queen bees to Brazil. He wanted to breed them with honey bees from Europe. He hoped to produce hardworking bees that would do well in Brazil's hot climate. While he was doing his experiments, some swarms escaped. Because killer bees are restless and hardworking, they spread quickly. The males mated with a local beekeeper's queens.

The new bees swarmed to the north and to the south. They invaded other countries.

## Killer Bees Hit the Newspapers

In Argentina, a school bus ran off the road and struck an electric light pole. No one was hurt in the accident, but there was a killer-bee nest in the pole. Forty-six students ended up in the hospital with stings. Another attack by killer bees sounds more like something from a movie than from real life. The bees took over

Weaver ants swarm over a tree branch. They use leaves to weave their nests.

a control tower at an airport. As you might guess, the man directing air traffic got out fast. It took a fire truck with a high-powered hose to get rid of the bees.

Killer bees have reached the southern United States. Cool winters should stop their northward spread. They sound terrifying, but it is very unlikely you'll ever be attacked by killer bees. If you are, don't try to fight them off. The best thing you can do is to run for your life. It's better to dive through bushes and trees than to stay in the open.

The people with the most to lose are those who depend on bees for their living. Besides selling honey, most beekeepers rent out their bees to pollinate crops and fruit trees. If killer bees take over a hive, this means trouble for beekeepers because killer bees are hard to work with. It's not just that they sting, they also swarm and fly off. Killer bees like to be on the move.

## Ants

There are many different kinds of ants, and most of them are weird. Some keep slaves; they raid other colonies and bring prisoners home to do the work. Some tend their own underground gardens; they plant mushrooms. Some store honey in the bodies of members of their group, turning them into live honey pots. But weirdest of all are the army ants. Like killer bees, these fierce ants always like to be on the move.

More than one hundred years ago, a naturalist exploring the jungles of Brazil was in a hut, when a strange rattling sound wakened him. As he reached for his gun, something bit his hand. Stabs of pain shot through his feet and ankles. He knew right away what was going on, he was being attacked by army ants.

**32**

Special worker ants, called repletes, act as living honey jars. The other worker ants beg for food when they are hungry.

The hungry insects swarmed up his legs. They tore at his skin with their quarter-inch jaws. Rushing out of the hut, he threw himself into a river. He pushed the ants off his body and waited for dawn.

The next day, the ants were gone, but they left behind a grim trail of death. The ground was covered with small skeletons. The ants had taken care of all the rats and mice in the village.

One of the strangest things about army ants is that they have no eyes. They find their victims by smell. Millions of them form a column a few feet wide, smelling out anything that is alive. The queen and grubs are carried along by the workers. Nothing stops the column—not even running water. When they come to a stream, they lock their legs together, and the front ants drift out into the water. When they touch the other bank, they hang on, forming a living bridge. The rest of the ants cross the stream on the backs of their comrades.

After a few weeks of raiding, the ants settle down for a spell of domestic life. They form a huge ball. It is just like a regular ants' nest, except that the walls are made of ants' bodies. There are tunnels and little rooms. The queen lives near the middle. She begins to lay eggs, and other ants tend to the larvae when they hatch. Soon the pupae from the last egg-laying become adults. Then the army gets ready for another raid.

## Locusts

Another rampaging insect is the locust. Locusts have stripped fields bare ever since people first started planting crops. Although they travel in gangs, locusts are not social insects. They have no queen, and they have no home. For a long time no one knew what happened to them in years when they didn't swarm; they vanished. Nobody ever saw just one locust.

The mystery was solved by

*Grasshoppers rest on a farm worker's back during a grasshopper outbreak in 1917.*

Boris Uvarov in 1921.[2] He found out that locusts lead a double life. Some years they are loners; other years they go around in gangs. When they join a gang, they take on a new look. They don't act as they did when they were on their own. They wear their gang colors, and they become greedier and wilder.

As loners, they look and act like other grasshoppers. Their green and tan colors blend into the background; they nibble on grass. They can live in this harmless way for generations. Then, when the weather and grass are right, more eggs are laid and those eggs all hatch. Young hoppers fight with other young hoppers for food, reacting to overcrowding. They all begin to eat more. Their color changes; instead of blending in with the grass, they are now red, yellow, and black. Their legs grow longer. Huge swarms of excited little hoppers cover the ground.

When the hoppers are full grown, they have wings and take to the air, flying downwind. The real journey has begun. By now there are so many that they darken the sky. They are like an invading army. Wherever they land, they strip the plants and trees bare, leaving a wide path of destruction.

Locusts fly wherever the wind takes them. Scientists from many countries banded together to fight them. They drew up battle plans; they used planes and chemicals. Then they realized that the best way to stop locusts is not to let them get started. Scientists now keep track of rainfall records all over the world. When the weather is right for locusts, they send out locust alerts. The aim is to keep those little hoppers from joining gangs in the first place.

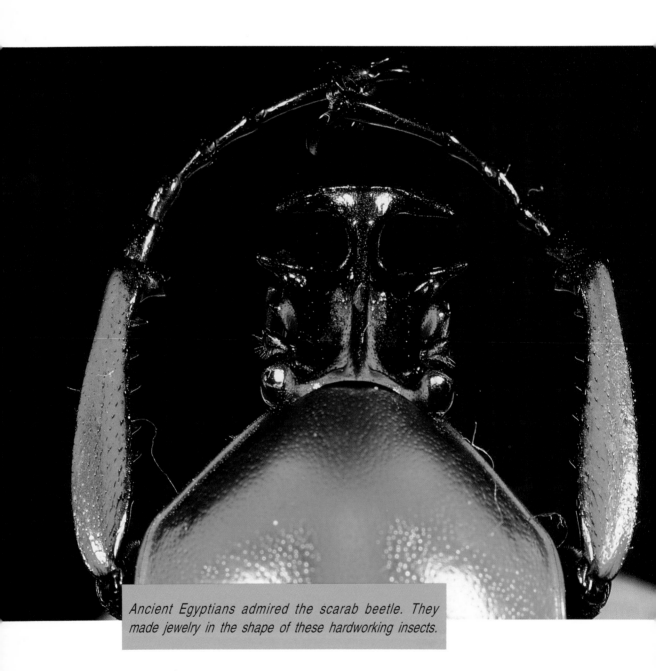

*Ancient Egyptians admired the scarab beetle. They made jewelry in the shape of these hardworking insects.*

# ☀5☀

# THE CLEANUP CREW

**B**eetles are in the order Coleoptera, the biggest order of insects. The name Coleoptera comes from the Greek words *coleos* (hard case) and *ptera* (wings). Their front wings form a hard case to protect the thin flying wings.

Human beings think that some beetles are harmful, and some are helpful. Scarab beetles, with their offbeat lifestyle, belong in the helpful group. They do their part to clean up the environment. A scarab is easy to recognize, because it is usually busy pushing around a ball of dirt. The ball can be bigger than the beetle.

The ancient Egyptians greatly admired scarab beetles. They often wore beetle-shaped jewelry with gems for wings. The scarab pushing its ball made them think of the great god Ra rolling the sun across the sky. When they made jewelry, they used pure gold for the ball. In real life, scarab beetles make their balls out of dung.

In Egypt, they mostly use camel dung. In other places they use horse dung or cow dung. In Africa, elephant dung is popular. Some of the scarab beetles in Africa are huge. Big beetles need a big supply of dung.

The obvious question is: Why do scarabs roll balls of dung all over the place?

Answer: Because they are looking for somewhere to bury them.

This leads to the next question: What happens to the dung balls?

Answer: Young scarabs eat them.

Scarab young, or larvae, are raised on dung. They like their dung fresh. The adults bury the dung so that it doesn't dry out. This is important in places like Egypt where the climate is hot and dry. Beetles rolling balls of dung around are looking for soft ground. When they find a place that suits them, they start to dig. When the hole is deep enough, they push the ball down into it. The female lays her eggs in the dung ball. Then the hole is filled in. After the eggs hatch, the larvae feast on the dung. When the larvae grow into adults, they crawl out of the ground.

The way scarab beetles pop out of the ground made the Egyptians think of another story about their gods: Seth murdered his brother Osiris by sealing him in a coffin. Osiris then became king of the dead. His son Horus later rose from the earth to rule the living world. The larva of the scarab beetle is like dead Osiris sealed in his coffin. The adult beetle then appears to claim its kingdom above the ground the way Horus did.

Scarabs find dung by its smell. Several beetles often work on

A scarab beetle rolls a ball of dung in search of a place to bury it.

the same cowpat. A scarab has a rake on its head that it uses to scoop up dung. While it works, it sorts out the fiber, only keeping the juiciest stuff. It shapes the ball against its body with its middle and back pairs of legs. While rolling the ball away, the scarab hangs on to it with its two front legs. Meanwhile it rotates the ball with its other four legs, so the ball ends up perfectly smooth and round.

## Beetle Experiments

A French naturalist named Jean Henri Fabre spent hours and hours watching dung beetles.[1] He noticed that some beetles prefer a life of crime to one of hard work. One beetle was happily rolling away his ball. Another zoomed down and landed on top of the ball, hoping to scare away the rightful owner. The first beetle set the ball rolling, trying to get the would-be thief to fall off. When this didn't work, the beetles joined forces and rolled the ball away together. The second beetle still had a backup plan. While the first beetle was digging a hole to bury the dung, he made off with the ball.

Fabre wondered how smart the beetles really are. He thought up some experiments to test their intelligence. Sometimes a small twig spears the ball, and the beetles have to work it loose. So Fabre nailed a dung ball to the ground with a straight pin. The beetle team that had been pushing the ball was puzzled when it wouldn't move. They walked around it for a while, then one burrowed under it like someone looking under the hood of a stalled car. Finally, it spotted the pin. It seemed to realize that the pin was the problem. Both beetles got under the ball and used their strong backs to lift it up. They raised the ball higher and higher. Soon they were standing on the tips of their claws. With one last heave, they pushed the ball off the top of the pin.

Next Fabre stuck a longer pin through the ball. Would one of the beetles think of climbing onto the other's back so that they could lift the ball even higher? The beetles weren't that smart! In fact, insects aren't smart at all. They operate by instinct. They can only solve problems if the answer is in their genes.

## Elephant Dung Beetles

Bernd Heinrich spent a lot of time in Africa watching beetles give elephant dung a working over.[2] Heliocopris, the biggest elephant dung beetle, doesn't roll dung away. It makes a hole right under the dung pile. It has strong digging blades on the front of its head and on the side of its front legs. It's built rather like a flying backhoe. The male and female beetles dig the hole together. When it's deep enough, the male tosses down bundles of dung to the female, who shapes them into balls. She lays an egg in each ball. The male then seals up the hole. The female stays down there. The hole becomes her tomb.

About two thousand different species of beetles in Africa live in dung. Some of them eat the dung right there. Others make dung balls and roll them away. A one inch-long beetle makes dung balls the size of a baseball. When Bernd Heinrich set up beetle races on smooth ground, he found that the fastest ones rolled at a speed of eight inches per second.

## The Australian Problem

Scarab beetles clean up a lot of dung. People found out how important they are when cattle were introduced into Australia. A cow puts out 12 dung pats a day, each weighing about 3.75 pounds. Australia's 30 million cows were producing 67,200 tons of manure each day.[3] Australia is a big country, but with that many cows and no beetles, it was in danger of being buried in manure. So beetles were brought in from Africa. The cleanup crew went to work and solved the problem.

It's not quite true to say that there were no dung beetles in Australia when cattle were first brought in; the kangaroo dung beetle was already there. This beetle doesn't like cow dung, which is just as well for the cows. It doesn't make dung balls as others do. It doesn't even wait for the dung to drop. It lays its eggs in a kangaroo's rectum; that way the young get their dung fresh. This also qualifies the kangaroo dung beetle for the prize for the strangest lifestyle in the insect world.

Even a science-fiction writer couldn't come up with something that weird!

Beetles, such as the scarab, help clean up the environment.

## Chapter 1

1. Sue Hubbell, *Broadsides from the Other Orders* (New York: Random House, 1993), p. xvii.

2. Robert H. Boyle, "Joy of Cooking Insects," *Audubon* (September/October 1992), pp. 100–103.

## Chapter 2

1. Lorus J. Milne and Marjorie Milne, *Insect Worlds* (New York: Charles Scribner's Sons, 1980), p. 96.

## Chapter 3

1. Howard Ensign Evans, *Life on a Little Known Planet* (New York: E. P. Dutton, 1968), pp. 164–165.

2. Karl von Frisch, *Ten Little Housemates* (New York: Pergamon Press, 1960), pp. 9–27.

3. L. H. Newman, *Man and Insects* (New York: Natural History Press, 1966), p. 122.

## Chapter 4

1. Laurence Pringle, *Killer Bees* (New York: Morrow Junior Books, 1990), p. 33.

2. L. H. Newman, *Man and Insects* (New York: Natural History Press, 1966), p. 132.

## Chapter 5

1. J. Henri Fabre, *The Insect World of J. Henri Fabre* (New York: Dodd, Mead and Co., 1966), pp. 93–107.

2. Bernd Heinrich, *In a Patch of Fireweed* (Cambridge, Mass.: Harvard University Press, 1984), pp. 101–109.

3. Karen Anderson, "Competition Between Dung Beetles," bachelor's thesis, Reed College, Portland, Ore. (1990), p. 28.

**antenna** (plural, **antennae**)—Feelers on the head of an insect.

**bug**—Not all insects are bugs. True bugs all belong to the insect order Hemiptera. They have sucking mouthparts and a leathery section on the upper wings.

**chrysalis**—The resting stage between a caterpillar and an adult butterfly.

**cocoon**—The envelope spun by some insects to protect the pupa.

**Coleoptera**—The insect order that includes all beetles.

**Diptera**—The insect order that includes all flies.

**entomologist**—A scientist who studies insects.

**exoskeleton**—An external skeleton that forms the hard skin of an insect.

**Hemiptera**—An insect order. True bugs are in the order Hemiptera.

**larva** (plural, **larvae**)—The stage of an insect between the egg and the pupa. Caterpillars, maggots, and grubs are all larvae.

**life cycle**—The stages from egg to adult.

**maggot**—Young stage of a fly. The word usually is used to describe a larva without legs.

**metamorphosis**—Changes in form and shape that take place between the time an insect hatches and the insect's mature adult stage.

**molt**—To shed skin to allow for new growth.

**order**—A major division in classification of organisms. Orders are divided into families, genera, and species.

**parasite**—An animal or plant that obtains food and shelter by living on or in another organism.

**predator**—A meat eater. The meat can be other insects.

**pupa** (plural, **pupae**)—The resting stage between the larva and the adult. During this stage the insect goes through a complete metamorphosis.

**species**—A group of organisms that closely resemble one another and are able to interbreed.

**spiracles**—Small holes along the body through which insects breathe.

**Kingdom:** Animalia
**Phylum:** Arthropoda
**Class:** Insecta
**Orders:** Thysanura (Silverfish, bristletails)
Ephemeroptera (Mayflies)
Odonata (Dragonflies, damselflies)
Plecoptera (Stoneflies)
Embioptera (Webspinners)
Phasmatodea (Walkingsticks)
Orthoptera (Grasshoppers, katydids, crickets)
Dermaptera (Earwigs)
Dictyoptera (Cockroaches)
Isoptera (Termites)
Psocoptera (Booklice, barklice)
Mallophaga (Chewing lice, bird lice)
Anoplura (Head lice, other sucking lice)
Hemiptera (True bugs: water striders, backswimmers, bed
bugs, stink bugs)
Homoptera (Cicadas, leafhoppers, aphids)
Thysanoptera (Thrips)
Neuroptera (Lacewings, antlions)
Coleoptera (Beetles, weevils)
Hymenoptera (Ants, bees, wasps)
Trichoptera (Caddisflies)
Lepidoptera (Butterflies, moths)
Diptera (True flies)
Siphonaptera (Fleas)

**Classification**

Facklam, Howard, and Margery Facklam. *Insects*. New York: Twenty-First Century Books, 1994.

Greenbacker, Liz. *Bugs: Stingers, Suckers, Sweeties, Swingers*. New York: Franklin Watts, 1993.

Heinrich, Bernd. *In a Patch of Fireweed*. Cambridge, Mass.: Harvard University Press, 1984.

Hubbell, Sue. *Broadsides from the Other Orders*. New York: Random House, 1993.

Kalman, Bobbie. *Bugs and Other Insects*. New York: Crabtree Publishing Co., 1994.

Milne, Lorus J., and Marjorie Milne. *Insect Worlds*. New York: Charles Scribner's Sons, 1980.

Mound, Laurence. *Amazing Insects*. New York: Alfred A. Knopf Books, 1993.

Parker, Steve. *Beastly Bugs*. Madison, N.J.: Raintree Steck-Vaughn Publishers, 1993.

Pringle, Laurence. *Killer Bees*. New York: Morrow Junior Books, 1990.

Snedden, Robert. *What Is an Insect?* San Francisco: Sierra Club Books, 1993.

# Further Reading

**Index**